11:11

KATHLEEN MELLO-NAVEJAS

11:11

A JOURNEY FROM DEATH TO LIFE

Charleston, SC
www.PalmettoPublishing.com

11:11 A Journey from Death to Life
Copyright © 2023 by Kathleen Mello-Navejas

First Edition

Hardcover ISBN: 979-8-8229-0368-5
Paperback ISBN: 979-8-8229-1502-2
eBook ISBN: 979-8-8229-1503-9

"The only way to make sense out of change is to plunge into it, move with it, and join the dance."

—Alan Watts

TABLE OF CONTENTS

FOREWORD

"When I think of 11:11, it's about the journey of life's adventures. This book is my mom's 11:11 journey through life with her father and family—but we can all relate to it one way or another.

While not everyone has a great childhood or relationship with their parents, this book shows you that life's journey is yours to take. There's laughter, magic, adventure through struggle, pain, and anger from all the times when your parents let you down, from the time you were a child to death.

As you read this book, you start thinking about your own lucky numbers in life. You will start to relate to the things that give you strength through a higher power to get through life's good and bad times.

As you read further, you will be reminded again this is your journey in life—not anyone else's—so make it good. Then as you finish the book, you realize in the end that all you have is your family. While people in your family may not like you or disagree with you at times, it's okay. And if you take anything away from this book, it's to always TAKE IT UP A NOTCH! *I love you to the moon and back!"*

—Your one and only Gina!

I first met Kathy's dad at the launch of Kathy's book Magic Money. *Writing these words I can replay the scene in my mind, a tender old man foiling over the need to drink his Ensure and him replying, "I have had enough." His wife said more fiercely, "You need to get your energy boost." It reminded me of my own great-uncle who came to live with us at the very end. He was very kind, like Kathy's dad, but also, as the age wore on, a bit cantankerous. Yet once the music began, Kathy's dad was dancing like no tomorrow. He even had quite a beat. The situation shifted, and people from the audience were coming up to congratulate the author on her work. Suddenly I got this sixth sense that her dad had a statement to make. I helped him out of his seat, his wife on the other side. Here we were in front of center stage, and there was silence as he forgot the words, yet then they came, "Kathy, I am just so proud of you. I have always known you could do it." Time suddenly stopped, and one could see the smile from Kathy to her father and back again. This moment was frozen in my mind.*

Months later I got the word he was in his last days, and the days were winding downward. As he left the world, there was a part of me that felt a loss as well. I was the one who pushed through the calls, "Is everything ok? How is Mom doing?" I am not part of the family, but that one event fast forwarded to part of the family.

It is therefore my honor to write this foreword.

Have you ever had one of those days where you asked yourself, "Why me, and how could this possibly happen?" and then you presented a book, The Journey from Death to Life.

It begins like a lesson book on what one may experience on the last road of life. Yet what separates this story from the rest is the quotes from different authors and writers, songs, and poetry that bring it all together.

They all say in academics, you can learn a lot about writing by skimming the foreword to know is this what I want, will this help me get to the path, and how do I go there.

Mom's perspective, father, children, struggle, and high road. Everything becomes a pattern to help self-reflect on your path and eventual destiny. Best of all we are left with the greatest gift in our own family, we love and disagree but come to see them anyway.

Chapter 1 takes a real look at how one views their father from youth to teen and adult. What adult is there who can't wait to leave the home raised and break out on rest. In youth we were color blind with rose glasses to disguise what is good and bad, and yet in adulthood we take another lens to take newer understanding. As one comes to the very end, they say our parents off regress to the state they entered the world, and we wonder how the transition may occur. Yet it offers a great lesson to appreciate every moment for what it's worth.

Chapter 2 handles the real situation, once the person expired to the human experience that runs the gamut of the rainbow in and the roles and character the different members of the family take on. In the chapter the pure, unfiltered beauty emerges, taking random incidence and transforming to great meaning. For a great spiritual walk brings forth a stranger who comes to teach a life.

Next is an instruction guide of what one may feel as they undergo the process. What is most special about the book is it becomes a tool of self-therapy. Do it yourself from reading the book. You are given the guideline, the lessons, the mantras, and finally the offer to join a workshop on helping people process death.

What truly separated this book from others is the way it unifies song, poetry, and personal experience to help anyone endure the unknown path when it comes to moving on. I hereby, with highest recommendation, know that all who read this will take a great deal of help to endure the passing of their loved one.

Rosalyn Kahn, Author, Humanitarian, and TV Host

I first met Kathy in 2023 at a hospital in Culver City. I had just been laid off my previous job, and Kathy was the Senior VP of the company that owns the hospital I was visiting. I was immediately drawn to her energy and positivity. She was very warm, kind, and a wealth of knowledge.

In her second book, 11:11: A Journey from Death to Life, *you take a walk with Kathy as she shares her experience, perspective, and challenges of the passing of her father. She describes a very clear picture of how she overcomes the inevitable—the preparation, process, and resolution. This book is like the hug we needed when we lose someone who is close to us. It is like the counselor beside you when we need to get aligned. This book is like your friend, your companion that whispers, "Take it in, take your time, stay strong, and push forward."*

Thank you, Kathy, for always enlightening me and guiding me with not just work, but also with my personal life. I am grateful for having her in my life, and I am honored to have written this foreword. I have nothing but happiness and gratitude for Kathy. Congratulations on another great piece.

Sincerely,
Percival "Patrick" Gonzaga

Many people discuss forgiveness, but I believe that it's wildly misunderstood. Yes, it's wise to forgive because the anger and bitterness only hurt us, but it's even deeper than that. Life is never one-sided; instead there are always negative and positive aspects to everything that happens to us. When a life event occurs, we decide what meaning to give it; in other words we choose to see the negative or the positive. A more balanced perspective would be to see both sides and thus avoid being one-sided.

So when we need to forgive someone, a wise action would be to see the blessings we received from that particular "negative" event. Did it make us stronger? More independent? Would we be the same person had that event not occurred? These are often challenging questions to ask, for when we are hurt or angry, we immediately go into blaming others. But if we believe we are creators, we can take 100% responsibility for our lives and ask ourselves, "How did we call this into our life?" and see all the gifts the event brought us.

Blaming others, not taking responsibility for our lives, and being unforgiving creates a low vibe that doesn't allow us to have the extraordinary life we are meant to have. Don't waste another minute in anger, bitterness, guilt, shame, or other low vibrations. Instead always focus on the blessings, the gifts that this life is constantly bestowing upon us. What if the Universe gave us beautiful life lessons to help us rather than hurt us?

This is the real Spiritual work. We can attend Church every Sunday, read ten thousand spiritual books, hire life coaches, climb Mt. Everest, and meditate with the most potent guru, but it all boils down to this: what is the energy we put into the world daily. I promise that life will be more complicated unless you constantly focus on the blessings and live a life of gratitude.

When you meet Kathy, you feel this beautiful energy I am talking about. She constantly focuses on her blessings and is obsessed with blessing everyone who crosses her path. She is one of the most generous beings I have ever met. I love how she loves people and wants to help them create magic in their lives. Kathy's smile lights up the room, and her happy energy is infectious.

Being in her presence alone is healing.

This book takes you through her journey. From her difficult childhood to her wild escape and the extraordinary life she has created today. Kathy has not only forgiven her childhood, she has also seen all the blessings and is grateful for all the "negative" experiences she has endured.

Kathy understands that they have made her the incredible human she is today. Would she be such an effective coach had she not been through all those complex challenges? Would Kathy be as non-judgmental as she is today? Would she be as loving to all human beings, regardless of their past? I can assure you not. All of our greatest gifts have come from our greatest pains.

This book will take you from death to birth, and you will understand the importance of loving who you are and creating an extraordinary life no matter what your past or present looks like. I am confident you will thoroughly enjoy it!

—Connie Costa, MA
Transformational Coach, International Speaker,
Published Writer & Sicily Travel Host

This simple book by Kathleen Mello-Navejas is going to be one of my new favs! Right next to How to Survive the Loss of a Love *by Melba Colgrove and Harold Williams (one that I have shared with others throughout my life).*

I enjoy self-help books, especially ones that can be read in a day and give you examples that you can identify with. Ones that will give you a knowing smile (been there) and some unexpected tears (OMG, done that!).

As an RN and Family Nurse Practitioner, I have worked with dying patients and their families for several decades. I am also one of the Baby Boomers currently attending funerals every couple of months.

No matter your religion or beliefs, this book is nonjudgmental and delivers the message—we will all go through the continuum of life and death. It is not an option. How you deal with the death of a loved one and the resultant emotions, actions, and memories can be affected. Expect your world as well as everyone else's in it to go haywire.

Kathleen shares her very personal experiences and steps in going through your own journeys. She also provides continued interventions that can be taken in the form of retreats and life coaching for those with special interests and needs.

I will gladly share this book with others! Thanks for sharing!

—Laurie J. Lee, RN, BSN, MSN, FNP-BC

INTRODUCTION

"Letting go gives us freedom, and freedom is the only condition for happiness. If, in our heart, we still cling to anything—anger, anxiety, or possessions—we cannot be free."

—Thich Nhat Hanh

THIS BOOK WASN'T just something I needed to write. It was something that I needed to acknowledge, focus on, and listen to as loudly as it was screaming inside me. You could call it a kind of "calling" pulling me into a vortex of feelings I call the "Zone"—where I needed to truly feel in order to heal.

It all began with my father's earthly ending. Just like Fitzgerald's book and the movie *The Curious Case of Benjamin Button*, I found myself wanting to start fresh and begin anew—as my father was taking his last breaths. Take baby steps and find brand-new, youthful perspectives as I started to mature. Watching my father die gave me the impetus to want to live in a whole new way—a kind of rebirth I could have never anticipated in a million years. *Death to Life*.

And the double trigger, in addition to his dying, was not the month of his passing. It was the timestamp on the clock: 11:11 p.m. That's when I realized he was gone. That's when they told me he had died. My sister and mother thoroughly disagreed (understatement!)

with me as to that time. They insisted that Dad died at 10:49 p.m. This has been a huge point of contention in my family, to put it mildly. I'll elaborate later.

What I ultimately realized was that it doesn't matter a hill of beans what the time of death happens to be (unless you're investigating some kind of crime, right?). But rather the time of death is a clarion call to life in an entirely new and often surprising way. It can even be shocking in spite of being anticipated. However it happens, whenever it happens, or whatever the circumstances of the passing of a loved one, we can anticipate the inevitable eruption of emotions in a startling volcanic stratosphere we never even knew we had deep within us.

We scream. We yell at each other. We sob. We laugh. We go silent. We go loud. We hug each other close. We push each other away. We love big. We hate big. We feel guilt over the relief. We feel deep regret. We feel peace. We feel disquietude. We feel lost. We feel found. And I felt all of those "feels" and a galaxy more experiencing the journey to my father's finish line.

So while much of this book documents my own personal exploration of the good, bad, and ugly of the trajectory of my father's death within me and my family, I also wanted this to be a kind of guide of self-discovery for you. If I could save you some of the drama I/we went through and help you see death as a life-giving adventure and a fresh start, I was going to give it my all.

The great master teacher Wayne Dyer, said, "Change Your Thoughts—Change Your Life." Of course he was right. What if we looked at the reality and ultimate passage of death (face it, my dears, we're all gonna die!) as a golden opportunity to grow younger in our spirit, in our perspective, in our understanding of what it means to truly be alive? I'm challenging you to please give it a try. Come, and join me on this rebirthing journey!

CHAPTER 1

THE BEGINNING OF THE END

"There will come a time when you believe everything is finished. That will be the beginning."

—Louis L'Amour

MY FATHER HAD been a monster for as long as I could remember—from my teen years until I fled out the window and into my new, wild life. He and I clashed wills and wits at a pivotal time in both of our lives—in which we were experiencing change.

A mighty mouse of a man—short in stature Dad was still huge in his power over me, my mother, and my siblings. A fierce Portuguese patriarch immigrant, my father was nine years older than my mother, who was Cajun French from Louisiana. She was just fourteen years old when she married my father, and she was still a teenager—merely sixteen years old when I was born.

At age eleven when more kids arrived in the family—my sister and brother—I was no longer the star, the single child, but now transformed—you could even say "catapulted" into becoming more of a reluctant babysitter and mother figure. And no matter what I did to nurture and protect my little family, that inner mantra I felt within me screamed loud and clear, I was "Not Enough."

Seen from my vantage point as an adult, I now see how painful my carefree life as a child had become at age eleven, when my mother birthed my sister and, eleven months later, my brother. After a huge gap of joy being the single star child, now I was forced to help my mother care for two babies 24/7. I was appointed the title of "live-in babysitter." And I wasn't a happy camper. How could this have happened?

After a joyful vacation to Portugal with my parents when I was eleven years old, miraculously, after not being able to conceive since she had me, my mother was pregnant—a joyful miracle on the one hand, but also a great source of angst, especially for my father. One baby girl arrived nine months later, and then, eleven months after my sister Anna Maria was born, out popped Daniel, my baby brother.

Now we were a family of five, which took a tremendous financial and psychic toll on my family—and contributed greatly to Dad's frustration and fear over how he was going to support us all. My parents were a hardworking, Depression Era couple; Dad was a gardener, and Mom ironed shirts with me working along beside her.

My mother was practically a child when my father married her. He hated being married to a child and having to raise a litter of more children. And she hated having to cater to her domineering father figure of a husband as well as juggle babies, forever scrimping and saving every last penny they made. Amazingly she managed to manage everything—but her unhappiness and resentment was buried deep in a volcanic well in her soul. In our own ways, we each hated our lives and each other.

I understand now from my grown-up perspective that the source of my "Not Enough" inner intonation was the result of being raised by two individuals whereby nothing was ever enough in their myopic and fear-based world. My mother, in particular, lived in a state of constant anxiety and distrust. I fought it, her, and them together like a lion in a cage and was as cantankerous and feisty in my longing to get out of that suppressive atmosphere as possible.

I drove them crazy. I longed to live a "More Than Enough" life. Not the suffocating one I was born into that was stomping out my entire being. Once I was eighteen years old and battled with them every single moment, fighting to be heard, seen, and understood, I had enough of living and being not enough in their claustrophobic world. Jumping out of my bedroom window, I fled from them forever. I truly was "born to be wild."

"BORN TO BE WILD"
(Song by Steppenwolf)

Get your motor runnin'
Head out on the highway
Looking for adventure
In whatever comes our way
Yeah, darlin' gonna make it happen
Take the world in a love embrace
Fire all of your guns at once
And explode into space
I like smoke and lightnin'
Heavy metal thunder
Racing with the wind
And the feeling that I'm under
Yeah, darlin' gonna make it happen
Take the world in a love embrace
Fire all of your guns at once
And explode into space

Like a true nature's child
We were born
Born to be wild
We can climb so high
I never wanna die
Born to be wild
Born to be wild
Get your motor runnin'
Head out on the highway
Looking for adventure
In whatever comes our way
Yeah, darlin' gonna make it happen
Take the world in a love embrace
Fire all of your guns at once
And explode into space
Like a true nature's child
We were born
Born to be wild
We can climb so high
I never wanna die
Born to be wild
Born to be wild

So now here I was—wildly me—back again and facing this man who had once metaphorically towered above me, blocking every aspect of myself—a man I both hated and feared as a teen and loved as a child. A fearsome patriarch I could never please; he triggered me to both tremble and fight back. It was time to unclench my fists. I could face him and breathe deeply. And now he couldn't hurt me anymore.

In fact he couldn't do anything anymore. He was dying. Prone in his bed in our home, with hospice caregivers buzzing around him like a revolving door, and my mother ever hovering to succor his needs—like she did all their seventy-plus years of marriage—this mighty man was now more childlike, and I couldn't believe it.

Mercy, help me—he was actually sweet! This wasn't the devil I had grown up with—the one who kicked me out the door when I was a teen, never to return—the man who was the source of every physical and mental roadblock in my entire life. How could that be? I stared at him non-stop as he would open and close his eyes—hold my hand—smile at me ever so benignly. This little man had become an angel!

In between his wailings of "I have to peee!" Dad was absolutely effusive in his gratitude for any of the small acts of kindness he was receiving from everyone. I heard him express, "God Bless You!" and "Thank you!" Seriously my father had become the dearest, sweetest man you could ever meet. And while we helped him pee, tucked him in, and comforted him, he would continually say our names over and over again like a chant, "Kathy, Anna Maria, Daniel, and my beautiful wife, Anna." Over and over again, he'd repeat our names. When my mother asked him why he was doing this, he would answer softly, "So I won't forget you."

My father had become this amazing angel at the very end of his life. And I was bereft. Instead of being filled with gratitude, I was struck dumb by these waves of deep regret and pain. This sweet man lying in front of me was now a stranger. He was gentle. He was kind. He was the personification of grace.

I didn't know him. Consequently I no longer knew who I was. Our dynamic had been so angst-filled up to now. What if—this question began bubbling up into my consciousness—what if he had always been some kind of angel, and I had pushed him deeper into the dark side? Was I the devil all along? Why could I never see the goodness in him? Which one of us brought the worst out of each other? I know I have this rude, nasty side that echoes my father in more ways than I'd like to admit. We even look alike. Were we twin spirits living/bringing out the worst in each other? Why couldn't we have shared such sweetness years ago rather than now? Nothing made sense.

But there was some gratitude in sharing his end game. I had been all packed and ready to go on a cruise with some of my girl-friends to celebrate my birthday. I was so excited, and I knew they had planned all kinds of fun surprises for me on the high seas.

I couldn't wait—and could just feel the sea breeze wafting around me, blowing through my hair. I mean my entire body was tingling, longing for that joyful freedom—the scent, sound, and peace of the sea mingled with the constant laughter of my friends with me. Oh! How I was so ready for it all. Even my mother was cheerleading me to go!

But when I told my boss, David, my cruise ship plans to set sail on the ninth of March, his words anchored me. Knowing that I was dealing with a sick parent, David asked me quietly, "Kathy, what about your father? What if he should die when you're far away in Panama? You can always travel someday, but you'll never be able to experience this time with your father. Of course you do what you want to do, but I think you'll regret it. Your family needs you now."

David's words touched me deeply. I knew he was not only right, but I felt so strongly that he was channeling a message from on High. I thank God I understood and heard the significance of it.

I bless you, David. You were so right because, almost immediately, my father took a turn for the worse. It was obvious he would pass while I'd be partying it up.

Torn between my girlfriends begging me to come with them and the voice inside that told me I'd regret leaving his bedside, I canceled the cruise. Even though my mother told me to go, he was going to die no matter what. "So enjoy your vacation." That's what she told me.

I wrestled with all the voices. The truth was I had left my father years ago. He had already died to me in a painful, cosmic death. I could have easily gone on the trip and justified my actions. And yet I couldn't. Something deep inside knew what David had told me was a truth I needed to face. I had to make peace with him, myself, and, in time, with my siblings as well. To this day I thank God for that decision.

So as my father began the daily journey closer and closer to his final destination, we would together watch family videos—ancient DVDs of so many memories I had long forgotten. This was Divine Intervention in so many ways. Because with each grainy video flickering before us, I was forced to see myself as a little girl.

Here I was, this sixty-nine-year-old woman, and I was watching me from another time and space. I was this adorable child who didn't appear mean or miserable. I was actually happy! Smiling. Laughing. Riding a horse. Running, pointing, and delighting in the World's Fair. Vacations in Portugal. Silent conversations we were all having together with such animation and excitement. I knew that was me eons ago, but where was I now? Where had that little girl gone? Was she still me?

My father would open his eyes and smile with each visual memory projected onto the screen. It was as if we were both having that "Life Review" I'd read about that we're supposed to have once we die. Only we were having them now, at this death-and-life precipice. Neither one of us appeared hateful or evil in those tiny feature films. We were a little family—two happy parents with their little girl having so much fun together. What, indeed, was the truth? I knew this was an Angel Orchestration.

My sister, who was eleven years younger than I, was always the caregiver in the family. Shy and retiring she never gave herself the chance to spread her wings, to know who she was in the world. She had appointed herself to be the devoted "Guardian Angel" of my parents, just like she was her entire life. Of course in contrast to me and my equally rebellious brother, Danny, she was the "Saint" to our "Devils." She was my parents' appendage—at their side to do their bidding 24/7, just as she was now more than ever as we took shifts watching our father die.

But before he left this earthly plane, I wanted to give Dad a clean exit. So while his heart was still beating, I needed to give him a fresh start. Literally. We stripped him of his clothes. His dirty diaper. The stench of death. And I began washing him down.

I know. Not all want to do this, and you really don't have to, but I needed to. I wanted my father to be sent off to Heaven smelling a hellava lot better than he did then. And while I washed my father, I got a chance to really see him. OMG. It was like I was looking at a male version of myself. His body, legs, hands, and feet. Mine. Exactly like mine. I was more like him in so many ways than anyone in my family, I discovered—maybe for the first time. So as I scrubbed him from head to toe, I stopped. His feet were in bad shape, so I smoothed them down with antibiotic cream. He was on the verge of death, right? Don't ask. This was for me.

We each organized ourselves to do what our own personal guts dictated. It seemed that we were being guided by an unseen "Source" choreographing our actions as we each faced this pivotal death/life passage.

My sister, Anna, was the calm in our family storm, as she always was. This was her lifetime role. Deeply sensitive and wise, she guided us to become more balanced, more tuned into what we were each facing. She prepared us for the inevitable next phase.

Beckoning us to stop our whirlwinding around Dad, Anna read us a piece by the esteemed Death Doula Sarah Kerr about what to expect when one dies. It very much helped me, helped us all, and I hope it will help you as well.

Expected Death ~ When someone dies, the first thing to do is nothing. Don't run out and call the nurse. Don't pick up the phone. Take a deep breath and be present to the magnitude of the moment.

There's a grace to being at the bedside of someone you love as they make their transition out of this world. At the moment they take their last breath, there's an incredible sacredness in the space. The veil between the worlds opens.

We're so unprepared and untrained in how to deal with death that sometimes a kind of panic response kicks in. "They're dead!"

We knew they were going to die, so their being dead is not a surprise. It's not a problem to be solved. It's very sad, but it's not cause to panic.

If anything, their death is cause to take a deep breath, to stop, and be really present to what's happening. If you're at home, maybe put on the kettle and make a cup of tea.

Sit at the bedside and just be present to the experience in the room. What's happening for you? What might be happening for them? What other presences are here that might be supporting them on their way? Tune into all the beauty and magic.

Pausing gives your soul a chance to adjust, because no matter how prepared we are, a death is still a shock. If we kick right into "do" mode, and call 911, or call the hospice, we never get a chance to absorb the enormity of the event.

Give yourself five minutes or 10 minutes, or 15 minutes just to be. You'll never get that time back again if you don't take it now.

After that, do the smallest thing you can. Call the one person who needs to be called. Engage whatever systems need to be engaged but engage them at the very most minimal level. Move really, really, really, slowly, because this is a period where it's easy for body and soul to get separated.

Our bodies can gallop forwards but sometimes our souls haven't caught up. If you have an opportunity to be quiet and be present, take it. Accept and acclimatize and adjust to what's happening. Then, as the train starts rolling, and all the things that happen after a death kick in, you'll be better prepared. You won't get a chance to catch your breath later on. You need to do it now.

Being present in the moments after death is an incredible gift to yourself, it's a gift to the people you're with, and it's a gift to the person who's just died. They're just a hair's breadth away. They're just starting their new journey in the world without a body. If you keep a calm space around their body, and in the room, they're launched in a more beautiful way. It's a service to both sides of the veil.

—Sarah Kerr,
Ritual Healing Practitioner
and Death Doula

It was nearly midnight, not quite, and I was sleeping in the other room when Anna called out to me, "Dad's taken his last breath! He's dead! Dad just died!" Running into the room, I was both shocked and furious! "Why didn't you call me in as he was dying?" I screamed at her. We were all crying.

Looking at the clock, I announced his passing at 11:11 p.m. "NO!" both my mother and sister fired back at me. "He died at 10:49! It wasn't 11:11!" Now we were in a bitch match over my father's dead body. I'm screaming, "11:11!" and the two of them are screaming back, "10:49!" The things you do and say at the onslaught of death. Grief can sometimes be a freak show.

In an instant I was reduced to that little girl I had witnessed in the videos—crying from the deepest of places I never knew existed in me. "Daddy! Daddy!" I sobbed over him. When did I ever call him "Daddy?" My inner child was wailing, wanting him back. I heard myself weeping over and over again, the little girl's longing for a father who was never there and now was truly gone forever.

Of course it really didn't matter—the exact time of Dad's death. But we were in the throes of grief, shock, denial—and the familiar game we seemed to play no matter what the topic. I played the bad guy, the extrovert, the bossy loudmouth; and they the more introverted, quieter ilk who ganged up on me—the black sheep of the family. I could say the sky was blue, and they'd want to kill me.

That was what we were used to. But the reality was one we could all agree upon.

Dad was dead. His body lay before us. A dead body. A corpse. A being that was once alive was now stiffening into a state of rigor mortis. But, surprisingly, I wasn't afraid nor repulsed. None of us were. Everything felt so peaceful. So blessed. The whole thing simply felt surreal. My mother lay down beside him. My sister prayed. I kicked into twelfth gear.

Now what to do?

I "saged" him—waving pure, fresh, calming scents of pine and lavender around and around over him. Was that for him or for us? I prayed out loud while I was saging him all over. Wafting away all the negativity, the stink, the fear of death in my desire, my hopes to create a transformative sweetness.

So, while I was saging my father's dead body, my mother was scrambling around like a mad woman, grabbing his clothes to dress him in his classy best in the morning. Time to meet Jesus in style.

"Ring the bells that still can ring
Forget your perfect offering
There is a crack, a crack in everything
That's how the light gets in."

—Leonard Cohen

CHAPTER 2

EMBRACING THE DARKNESS

"We live, embrace, and put to rest our dearest things, including how we see ourselves, so we can resurrect our lives anew."

—Mark Nepo, poet and teacher, *The Book of Awakening*

MOTHER STAYED BESIDE Dad's body all night, praying the rosary. But by 9 a.m. she was all about getting him dressed and ready to get the hell outta Dodge. The poor lady was thoroughly exhausted—totally depleted. At eighty-five years old (Dad was ninety-four), she had catered to that man her entire life—ever since she was a teenager. Now she was free.

His clothes were all laid out, pressed, neat, and ready for him. An entire snazzy outfit—complete with his vet cap that he was so proud to wear. "He's ready to go!" she nearly shouted. She could have said, "I'm done. I'm unchained. I don't have to do one more thing for this man!" In spite of myself, I burst out laughing. I mean if I was married to that guy for seventy-and-a-half years, I'd be ready to boot him out the door, too!

But while we waited for the coroner to arrive, I gazed at my father in sort of a state of disbelief. Was he truly dead? I pushed him. No response. How could that be? This multi-dimensional being who had been the thorn to my rose was a popular and well-loved landscaper and gardener all his life designing beautiful topiaries on lawns everywhere.

His great Portuguese pride was legendary, along with his double pride in being a vet. He was loved by many—a fierce, loyal, and mighty man. But now he was lifeless. I stared at him and looked at every feature as objectively as possible. And it occurred to me then that what I was looking at was the shell in which this spirit who had been my earthly father once lived. This shell resembled my father; however, the occupant was no longer there. The outer encasement we call a body had metaphorically cracked open to let the light of the Inner Spirit go free.

The realization of contemplating that the Light from within and Above cannot get into us or out of us until there is a cosmic crack to open it all up truly stunned me. I don't believe we have to die in order for the Light to enter us. We can let down our guard, open ourselves to vulnerability, but most of all SURRENDER and release. That's when we can make it possible for light to enter—as well as leave—our entire being. Death to Life. Or is it more—Death to LIGHT?

My father had surrendered in death what he could never do for me in life. He became the light. And, ironically, as I was witnessing him in front of me—so was I.

Why in the world, I wondered, couldn't we be each other's shining light while we are alive?

"I SURRENDER ALL"

All to Jesus I surrender
All to Him I freely give
I will ever love and trust Him
In His presence daily live
I surrender all
I surrender all
All to Thee
My blessed Savior
I surrender all
All to Jesus I surrender
Make me, Savior, wholly Thine
Let me feel Thy Holy Spirit
Truly knowing that Thou art mine
I surrender all
I surrender all
All to Thee
My blessed Savior
I surrender all (ooh)
Ooh
Ooh
Ooh
All to Jesus I surrender
Now I feel the sacred flame
Oh the joy of full salvation
Glory, glory to his name
I surrender all
Oh, I surrender all
All to Thee
My blessed Savior
I surrender all
Oh, I surrender all

Oh, I surrender
Oooh, yeah

Songwriters: Anson R. Dawkins / Derek Clark / Eric D.
Dawkins / Judson Wheeler Van Deventer / Winfield Scott
Weeden
I Surrender All lyrics © Capitol CMG Publishing, Spirit Music
Group, Universal Music Publishing Group

EXIT LIFE

"Life is a spark between two identical worlds—the darkness before birth and the one after."

—Irving Yalom

It was time to call the mortuary and transport my father. Yikes. That's a tough moment, trust me. Just as I walked outside to breathe fresh air into my lungs and get something from my car, this big green van pulled up with "Brings Mortuary" on the side.

Within moments I was leading the driver into the house. I swear it was like a scene from the movie *Beetlejuice*. It couldn't be weirder. This tall, scary-looking, gangly young guy dressed entirely in black with straggly hair down to there, completely tatted, painted black nails—I mean we're talking Goth times infinity—is following me, pushing a gurney. I couldn't help notice that one of his tattooed hands had "Exit Life" inked onto it. I asked him about it.

He said that it reminded him of his purpose. "You know I've done a lot of things in my life; had a lot of jobs. But what I'm doing now feels right. I know this is where I'm supposed to be. I have a calling dealing with the dead," he answered in barely a whisper. And he continued explaining, "I just feel close to people and their families, especially at the time of death. I feel God called me to deal with death, to go to people's homes, take the bodies, talk to the families—and make everyone feel it's all okay. Maybe I'll even be an embalmer someday. I don't know. But I do want you to know that we will take very good care of your father. We will handle him with care and love."

I soon realized that our Goth guy was an Angel in Disguise. Gentle, compassionate, and emanating empathy, his entire presence immediately calmed us. Explaining every aspect of what was about to ensue, he told us that once we moved the body, it could make some noise because of the bottled gasses in the gut and might leak fluids. All normal. Then as he gently placed our father in a body bag on the gurney, he took out this beautiful quilt and wrapped him in it.

You could hear the united gasp of my family as we saw that quilt. It was the exact duplicate of my grandmother's quilt! My mother couldn't believe it when she sobbed, "Oh my God! That's the same pattern as my mother's quilt!" This wasn't just a coincidence. This was Destiny. My grandmother was a gifted quiltmaker. Hugging my mother tightly, tears streaming down my face, I said, "Your mother is with him." And she said, "Exactly."

Oh, the comfort we all felt at that moment. Ironically I had already signed up for a quilt-making class in a few months with an amazing woman I had met while I was trekking The Camino de Santiago* in Spain last year (I had walked The Camino a year prior to that as well, with seven of us on a "Girls Gone Wild" trek together. Last year five of us wild women hiked it again. Both times we felt God's Presence guiding us along the way. It's a very profound journey, and I highly recommend it to everyone.)

The woman I had met on this last Camino walk I'm convinced was another Master Teacher. Her name is Sandy Bonsib, from Bloomington, Indiana—once a total stranger, now another Angel in my life. I still get chills when I recall our initial meeting and meaningful conversation in which she told me she was a folk-art teacher and quilt maker. As a token of our connection in the middle of that Camino road, she gifted me a small quilt square. It was so lovely. I still cherish it.

And I told her that my grandmother was a quilt maker. Her reply to me was as if an angel was speaking directly to my soul. "You must continue your grandmother's legacy, my dear. That's what we women do when we quilt. We are keeping our ancestors alive in our hands and hearts linked together from generation to generation." I understood. "This is how you keep your grandmother and all those before and after her alive."**

"We stitch together quilts of meaning to keep us warm and safe, with whatever patches of beauty and utility we have on hand."

—Anne Lamott

So triggered by the memories of that quilt hugging my dad and giving us each such comfort, our little family tribe rolled him out of the house and into the awaiting van. My mother on the left of the gurney. My sister on the right. I was at his feet in the front, helping pull it forward. A somber procession handing off my father from Death to Life—I believe it was a Rebirth for him and for each of us in so many ways.

It was at that moment when the van doors were opened and we were about to slide Dad in when I called attention to the number painted on the back. It was as if it was shouting out loud. "Look at me! Do you get it?" The number was 23—a very significant number for all of us. Again there are no accidents.

*The Camino de Santiago, also known as the Way of St. James, is a renowned pilgrimage of medieval origin that sees pilgrims journey to the Cathedral of Santiago de Compostela in Galicia in the northwest of Spain. Legend has it that the remains of the Apostle St. James the Great were buried in the Cathedral and discovered by a shepherd in the ninth century. The city of Santiago is named after St. James: Santiago de Compostela means St. James of the Field of Stars.

**Quilts represent connections, family, stability, and expression of the creative spirit that allowed women to overcome hardships. Quilts are recognized as symbols of these feminine and family values. Quilts represent connections, family, stability, and the creative spirit of overcoming hardships. They are recognized as symbols of feminine and family values. Quilts, made with multiple layers of fabric, were traditionally sewn together using knots. Researchers discovered quilts with unusual knot patterns, suggesting they may have conveyed travel patterns to escaping slaves. This knotting method had roots in African belief systems, where five knots were tied in cloth for protection from spirits. Quilts, with their patterns and symbols, served as a means for enslaved individuals to communicate and share their stories when they couldn't read, write, or openly talk.

Quilts have a rich history beyond providing warmth. They tell stories through their designs and have been part of cultures worldwide for centuries. They hold personal family histories, secret narratives, and lessons for the world to see and remember. Quilt designs can represent family memories and are often made with upcycled materials like t-shirts. They can also be symbols of community resilience, as seen in the famous quilts of Gee's Bend, Alabama. Created by generations of artists, many with ancestral ties to slavery, these quilts showcase distinct improvisational styles. They have gained recognition through national art tours and postage stamps, allowing the quiltmakers to share their stories with the world.

CHAPTER 3

THE TURNING POINT: LOOK FOR THE SIGNS

"I believe in everything until it's disproved. So, I believe in fairies, the myths, dragons. It all exists, even if it's in your mind. Who's to say that dreams and nightmares aren't as real as the here and now?"

—*John Lennon*

NOW FOR ME who completely believes in the Miracle of Angels and a Higher Force—God, The Universe, Holy Spirit, Jesus—it gives me great comfort in feeling/seeing some powerful Presence on my path. Key Signs along the way affirming my Life's Journey. Something Bigger orchestrating/overseeing us.

Some of you may discover Signs that are transformative in ways that mean something to you—through nature, animals, found objects, melodies, scents, words. I cannot encourage you enough to be aware of them. Appreciate them. In my world, when they show up, those are the evidence of Higher Forces reminding you that they're there for you, that you're not alone, that they hear and see you. If something meaningful appears, bless it and see it as a blessing.

Still I realize many of you don't believe any of that and think everything is a crapshoot—the luck or unluck of the draw. An accident. A coincidence. And seriously that's fine by me. Whatever gives us solace in this noisy earthly existence, right?

But the elephant—or should I say the ELEVEN—in the room upon my father's death was a true wake-up call for me. Yes, my sister and mother were screaming at me that Dad died at 10:49, not 11:11. Did they purposely withhold calling me into the room as he took his last breath? Was the whole time-lapse calling me into the room at the exact moment of his death intentional on their part? Were they in shock? What took them so long to tell me? Did it even matter when they finally shouted to me that he had passed, and I saw the time as 11:11?

That number screamed louder in my psyche than those banshee women in a rage—Mother spewing, "I HATE THAT GAWDAMN 11:11!" over my insistence over his time of death. Mother raged on, her face a fury of fire red. "EVERY TIME I'LL SEE THAT '11:11,' I'LL BE PISSED THINKING YOU'RE NOT IN REALITY! YOUR SISTER WAS THERE, AND IT WAS 10:49!" she fumed at me. As usual my concerns, my perspective, my voice simply did not matter. Typical.

Did I see the 11:11 as my father's Heavenly Hug, wanting peace between us over how he treated me when I was a teenager—beginning with the profound cataclysm of change that happened when I was eleven years old?*** We'll never know.

But here's what I do know and believe about 11:11. When you see that time, 11:11, whether it's on a piece of paper, a license plate, a phone number, on a sign, etc.—angels are trying to tell you something. It's time to connect with your intuition. Whether your life is about to change for the better or it's signaling you to take action for a positive outcome, have faith! A good transformation is near.

So while I was, and still am, deeply moved by the meaning of 11:11 showing up when it did, I was also struck by the additional Angel Signs at that time. Continuing with that number 23 on the back of the mortuary van.

So this is why I felt the Angels were doing all they could for us to understand completely that we were more a unit than we could ever see from our vantage point. The numbers "11" and "23" are woven throughout my family like grandma's quilt! And here's something else to add to the magical mix: 23:11 is the twenty-four-hour military clock equivalent of 11:11 p.m.! Military time means the twenty-four-hour clock time convention (without the colon) between hours and minutes is **2311**. So you can see why I hold steady to all things 11:11 involving my father (who was the pride-filled epitome of all things military) AND "23"—a biggie in my family.

My sister was born on *June 23*. My brother's birthday is *May 23*. My birthday is *March 23*. My sister and I are *11* years apart. And she and my brother are *11* months apart.

No matter how dysfunctional we might be, I see my family and me as a "meant-to-be" on so many levels—and this is helping me learn so many lessons about myself. I'm not a victim. I'm a student. And also a teacher. We all are. That's why we're here. To absorb. To learn. To teach. Everything and everyone in our lives teaches us something about ourselves if we stand back, be still, listen, and learn. We're meant to take these learned lessons and share them with others. It's as simple as that, I promise you.

"Grieving"
Has no clock
Has no manual
Has no timetable
Has many ups and downs
Is different for everyone
Is done your way
Is done on your own time frame
Is something we have to work through
Is something we all have to live with
Our loved ones who have crossed over are Okay
Our loved ones are still very much with us
Our loved ones know the pain we are going through
Our loved ones do the best they can to help us
Our loved ones want us…in time to be happy again
Our loved ones only have the greatest love for us
Always remember the separation from our loved ones is
only temporary. We will all be re-united with our loved ones,
when our own journey has been completed with great joy and the
greatest love you can ever imagine.

Spirit always has our backs.
They're always with us. Always watching, supporting, and
Nurturing us from the other side.
They are always trying to connect with us by sending us
messages and signs but it's up to us to look for and
acknowledge them.
Stop trying to talk yourself out of seeing these signs or
chalking them up as coincidences.
Coincidences do not exist—we're just not always
paying attention so when we notice that something
lines up perfectly, we convince ourselves that it must
be a fluke.
Let's remember that everything happens in divine timing.
The universe does nothing on accident and does not make
mistakes.
Next time you notice a sign, message, or "coincidence,"
acknowledge it
by thanking Spirit and ask yourself what it could mean for you.

Take these messages and signs from Spirit and
ask yourself what it could mean for you.
Take these messages and signs from Spirit with so
much love and allow them to guide you on your highest path.
—Victoria Tippett, The Limitless Woman

According to Hans Decoz of Numerology.com, "The number 11
represents instinct and is the most intuitive of all numbers. It is
your connection to your subconscious, to gut feeling and knowledge without rationality." It's also the number you'll see often see
when you're about to experience a spiritual awakening, "or rebirth
of some sorts," says Imelda of TrustedPsychicMediums.com.

Within Protestant Christianity, especially Pentecostal movements, the number 11 or 11:11 has *been associated with transition*. In numerology some New Age believers often associate 11:11 with chance or coincidence. Others believe that it is a signal from your angels, as they're letting you know they're close by. However, in other cases, 11:11 is seen as a new beginning or that you are on the right path going in the right direction.

CHAPTER 4

SITTING SHIVA

"Life is simple. Everything happens for you, not to you. Everything happens at exactly the right moment, neither too soon nor too late. You don't have to like it...it's just easier if you do."

—Byron Katie

MY MOTHER HAD taken care of it all—from contacting the priest to the mortician to arranging the mass to the burial. I mean the whole enchilada. She wouldn't let any of us pay for a thing. This little lady didn't want her kids to have to carry the burden of their parents in any way.

This from two people who scraped together every last coin they had, worked hard all their lives, and still lived in the same house they had purchased some seventy years ago. From living a mantra of "Not enough" all their lives, they gave us more than enough at this juncture. We really didn't have to do a thing because our mother taught us each a lesson on how to plan, organize, and take care of all the finances ahead of time. We were very impressed and, yes, very grateful. But we were each processing Dad's death differently. To say the least.

Mom was now in a full-on hysteria attack, screaming at the top of her lungs in one room. She'd truly blown a fuse. My sister and I had an "I hate you, I love you" shriek-a-thon at each other. Both were ganging up on me over the 11:11 vs. 10:49 time! I think we all had a psychotic breakdown in tandem. We shouted everything we ever wanted to say to each other since the beginning of time.

And my son, Anthony, who had been dealing with his own demons, suddenly became the wisest, most calming being in the room and was doing all he could to put out the fire, trying to out-shout us—"Ladies, ladies, calm down. Calm down, Mom. It's okay, Grandma. You have to be kind to each other. You have to be loving to each other. Please stop yelling."

Anthony—with the matted hair dreads and wrestling with his own inner schizophrenia monsters—was the one who finally was able to douse our fiery tantrums. We were completely wrung out, so weary and spent from fighting all the rage that had bubbled up when Dad died.

The sudden quiet in the room seemed louder than our screaming voices moments before. Now Mom found her breath at last and had a request, "I want all my children to go together to the mortuary. I want us all to come together. I want you to be peaceful. I want you to get along. I WANT PEACE! Do you understand, Kathy?" I was being thrown the gauntlet. My challenge, my impossible mission if I were to accept it, was to shut my mouth and BE PEACEFUL, GAWDAMMIT! I got the message.

Swallowing my pride and, yes, some laughter, I told myself to behave. It was time to conform with this little tribe, even if it was for just our brief moment together. I asked my son if he wanted to come with us, and he bowed out, "No, thanks, Mom. I'll stay here with the dogs."

TABLE FOR FIVE:
SITTING SHIVA AT RED LOBSTER

"We are injured and angry, scared and sad. Some families, like some couples, become toxic to each other after prolonged exposure."
—Jonathan Tropper, *This is Where I Leave You*

There is a Jewish tradition called "Sitting Shiva," which is a period of mourning right after the burial service. Lasting seven days and held in the home of one of the family members, it's a time for friends and family to visit those in mourning, offering their condolences and providing comfort. It's also a time to openly express sorrow, discuss the loss of the loved one, and slowly heal and uplift together as they reenter society.

I loved learning about this tradition, especially when I first saw it dramatized in the hilarious 2014 movie *This Is Where I Leave You.* Both funny and touching, the movie depicts four grown siblings forced by their mother (Jane Fonda) to return to their childhood home and live under the same roof for one entire week. Along with their far too oversharing mother, the siblings, their spouses, execs, and might-have-beens, the result is sheer chaos and the kind of truth most of us can relate to in many ways.

I just couldn't help thinking about that movie and the Shiva tradition when my mother insisted—not unlike Fonda in the movie—for us to gather together for a family meal. Okay, it was *before* Dad's burial, and it wasn't exactly tucked into one of our homes. Mother had it all planned out. "I would like all my children to go together to the mortuary. And I want this to be PEACEFUL! DO YOU HEAR ME, KATHY? I want you to all get along!" She might have screamed that at us—me in particular.

So I'm talking myself off the ledge, telling my inner belligerent pushback voice to please behave. Anthony stayed home watching the dogs. And for the first time in what seemed forever—we were in one tiny place together, crowded inside the car—with my mother, sister, and brother (who hadn't spoken to me in years), like trying to gasp for air in a submarine. Talk about claustrophobia.

So we arrived at the mortuary together, carrying the neatly pressed clothes for Dad that she had at the ready, including his coveted veteran's hat. And we handed over the necessary paperwork Mother had already filled out and paid for on her own. Saw the casket that Dad had already picked out long before this. It was all organized and seamless, thanks to Mother's orchestration of everything.

Ordered to keep our (my) mouth shut by Mom and go over all the details together with the mortuary manager—a sweet and gentle guy—we amazingly checked off each step together to reach a collective agreement on how the whole thing would happen. And then Mom said it was time to have lunch. She'd planned for that, too.

Ironically we all hadn't sat together at one meal for as long as I could remember. The chosen place, dictated by Mom, was Red Lobster. No questions asked. Done and done. We just nodded our affirmative and found ourselves facing each other in a plastic-padded booth at the restaurant. Sitting Shiva staring at a bunch of lunch menus while shoulder to shoulder with our miserable family. We were the quietest we'd ever been in our entire lives. Barely breathing. Each afraid to say a thing in case we blew up in some kind of fury.

I chanted this inner mantra to myself, "Kathy, be civil. Don't say a thing." And it worked. I had temporarily changed the Bitch Channel I seemed to tune into with my family to a sweet tune I never even recognized. So we all began a bright banter—a friendly chit-chat that kept everything light—like a balloon being passed from one to the other before it landed or burst.

I was praising our mother on how, after years of hard work and saving every last penny, she had paid for Dad's entire funeral herself. It all was quite impressive. "Well, I don't want to leave my children with any bills," she answered softly. "When I was raising you, I was forced to hide money from your father to pay bills and any extras you may need. He wasn't nice to me. He'd get mad all the time." How I remember Mom's constant words throughout my childhood: "Don't tell your father." Now her pain was bubbling to the surface. All those years of burying her resentment toward and being dominated by him, at last she was able to actually bury the man for real. This was one transformative moment. Hell, "Shiva Happens!"

At the end of our Red Lobstering, she took out her credit card and attempted to pay for the whole meal. Of course she resisted any offers we had to contribute. But I wasn't having it. Even though I realized that her need to pay for everything was recompense for her being a slave since she was a child bride. This was her chance to pay it forward. I was blown away, but I somehow convinced her that this one time I was going to pay for this bill.

Grabbing her hands, my eyes brimming, I begged her, "Mom, after all the years you and Dad struggled so hard to take care of us kids, and you have taken care of every single financial arrangement now, this is the least I can do. Please let me do this for you." After all how many times had I personally helped so many others pay for their funerals, donating to legions of Go-Fund-Me's for the burials too pricey to be financed? And here was my little mother who had scraped together a lifetime of her savings to do it all with her head held high, depending on no one. Every. Single. Aspect of Dad's final exit was taken care of. We kids didn't have to do a thing but show up and say our goodbyes. And so we did. But I insisted that I take care of our Red Lobster Shiva Lunch. I must have outyelled her because she reneged. Amazing.

CHAPTER 5

FINAL FAREWELL

"In the midst of death, life persists. In the midst of untruth, truth persists. In the midst of darkness, light persists."
—Mahatma Gandhi

THE MOMENT HAD arrived for us to face our father's burial. In our family we wanted a casket burial, as per my parents' wishes. But I know many of you have other plans for how you or your loved ones want the end to be orchestrated—such as cremation and spreading ashes in the wilderness, rivers or oceans, or other places that hold meaning for you. Others want to be mulched into compost, buried inside trees, immortalized in urns, melded into sculptures of glass, and so much more.

Truly all that matters is that you and your loved ones feel peace in the parting—and the death ritual is more life-giving than maudlin or scary. Your officiant should be someone you care about and respect—be it a beloved family member, a dear friend, or a religious leader—from a pastor to a priest to a rabbi to an imam to a shaman, and so many others—including a midwife! Wouldn't that be cool having a midwife "rebirth" you or your loved one when the body dies? I kind of love that idea. But truly "in the end/beginning," it's all up to you and your family.

That's how we approached Dad's endgame. When I spoke to our priest, I felt very much at home with him and the wisdom of his heart. Father Mark is a good man. Right away I told him that a long time ago, in my youth, I had wanted to be a nun. And it was at this church that I was most influenced by the wonderful Sister Jonesie. She was so full of life and vitality and very much like the Whoopie Goldberg nun in the 1994 movie *Sister Act* that I was inspired to be just like her. Until I visited the convent and was told that it would take five years of a lot of hard work and kneeling 24/7 prayers when I would ever be able to travel the world like Sister Jonesie did.

The Mother Superior at the convent was a dour taskmaster without an ounce of *joie de vivre* in her entire body, mind, or spirit. Calling her horrible was an understatement! I couldn't escape that place fast enough. That's what I told the priest at our church. "You see, Father, I wanted so much to travel the world and do good like Sister Jonesie but never made it." Well, that priest looked straight into my eyes and, with a gentle smile, said, "I'll bet you've traveled all around the world extensively, haven't you?" I must have gasped, "How do you know that, Father?" He answered softly, "Because I heard you, my dear. You didn't have to become a nun to do what you love in your travels to help many. You're doing God's work simply by being who you are." His words went straight to my soul. He was right. I am doing God's work; I love healing and giving hope to people. My own personal struggles have fueled my life's purpose to support others in myriad ways.

So that was the beginning gift of our journey to bury my father. Everything continued to fall into a peaceful place. (With the exception, of course, of writing and publishing the Obituary. I conferred with the whole family on the details, but in the end, I still added that 11:11 death time, which set off a whole new fury with my mother and sister, tsunami-ing me the likes of which I still haven't recovered. ARE YOU KIDDING ME?)

Still, besides that fiasco, which remains one frigging open wound in my family, the funeral went on with blessed ease. I'm used to heading big events, so I jumped in and organized the entire service, along with precious assistant Jocelyne, my granddaughter, who did an exemplary job of helping me plan the Mass, the Obituary, Eulogy, Closing—all of it. My sister sang a beautiful song entitled "The Other Side," which was so moving. She had us all in tears.

"THE OTHER SIDE"
Don Conoscenti

I'm over on the other side where life and death
softly divide
I left my skin and bones behind now I'm over on
the other side
Can you feel me there with you?
My breath is gone but I'm not through
I loved you then and I still do from over on the
other side
I can fly, really fly
Below the earth, all through the sky
Tell 'am all I did not die
I'm just over on the other side
It's good here on the other side
The sweetest songs, the bluest skies
Thank you for the tears you cried, but it's good
here on the other side
I can fly

The world is smaller than a needle's eye
Where life and death softly divide
When you leave your skin and bones behind
I'll be waiting on the other side
I can fly, really fly
Below the earth, all through the sky
Go tell 'em all I did not die
I'm just over on the other side

The song, from the album Paradox of Grace, *was submitted by Don Ackerman and Jean Detrick, Norwood.*

Each of our family wanted to say something about Dad. I was afraid that the holdout would be my brother, Danny. He and our father had a long-standing standoff. If Dad was tough on me, he'd been a tyrant to my brother. There was definitely no love between them—which is a huge understatement. And the same went for me. Danny held a deep resentment toward me for years after I apparently stepped over the line to save him, and he—sending me double messages—didn't want my help. Oh well. I still would do the same damn thing. But whatever.

Anyway, holding my breath, I asked Danny if he would be willing to speak. As the only son, it felt most appropriate that he should do the Eulogy. And surprisingly he agreed. He needed to heal from the regrets and anger that simmered within him, literally "burying" his pain to be free from a father who didn't know how to be a father. Death to Life.

In the end Danny's words touched us all deeply. Because he only inferred the stopgap between him and his father and featured a happy moment instead. Danny shared with us a childhood memory of when he had wanted to mow our lawn, and at eight years old, that would have been a far more daunting task than a little kid could take on. So Dad stood behind him and helped his young son push the lawnmower. It was a life highlight for the little boy that he never forgot. He needed his father's encouragement and support, and that meant the world to him.

My brother's speech was short, sweet, and gracious. I hoped it would have helped him mend that festering fury in his tormented soul. Maybe this was a start. Danny's final words as he ended his talk were my favorites. He said, "Our father was short in stature, but his name was not. Dad was 'Carlos Rebelo Fagunda De Mello.' A big name for a short guy." I thought that was profound. Short and sweet.

I requested to give my talk at the Closing of the service. I thanked everyone—so many friends, many who had traveled from far away to support us and personally comfort me, doctors and co-workers and tons of team members from everywhere, plus children, grandchildren, and great-grandchildren—all there to honor our father and us.

It was so heartening to see and feel that overwhelming support. I felt so blessed. Culminating my Closing speech, I singled out my siblings, thanking them with all my heart for their sacrifice and love, and reiterated Dad's poignant chant memorizing each of our names, "Kathy, Anna Maria, Daniel, and my beautiful wife, Anna." Practically chanting our names over and over again before he passed. It was a sacred time for our family. And, most of all, I discovered as we prayed around him that although we could have never believed it, he truly was an angel in disguise. My final offering to the congregation was for everyone to listen to a beautiful song that reinforced the fact that angels are among us, welcoming our father home.

"ANGELS AMONG US"
Song by Alabama

I was walking home from school on a cold winter day
Took a shortcut through the woods, and I lost my way
It was getting late, and I was scared and alone
But then a kind old man took my hand and led me home
My mama couldn't see him, oh, but he was standing there
And I knew in my heart, he was the answer to my prayers
Oh, I believe there are angels among us
Sent down to us from somewhere up above
They come to you and me in our darkest hours
To show us how to live, to teach us how to give
To guide us with the light of love
When life held troubled times and had me down on my knees
There's always been someone to come along and comfort me
A kind word from a stranger to lend a helping hand
A phone call from a friend just to say I understand
But ain't it kind of funny at the dark end of the road
That someone lights the way with just a single ray of hope
Oh, I believe there are angels among us
Sent down to us from somewhere up above
They come to you and me in our darkest hours
To show us how to live, to teach us how to give
To guide us with the light of love
They wear so many faces, show up in the strangest places
To grace us with their mercy in our time of need
Oh, I believe there are angels among us
Sent down to us from somewhere up above
They come to you and me in our darkest hours

To show us how to live, to teach us how to give
To guide us with the light of love
To guide us with a light of love

Source: Musixmatch

Songwriters: Don Goodman / Becky Hobbs

Angels Among Us lyrics © Sony/ATV Tree Publishing

CHAPTER 6

TIME TO HEAL:
A NEW BEGINNING

"In the midst of winter, I found there was, within me, an invincible summer."

—Albert Camus

IT WASN'T MY first choice for us to gather for the post-funeral reception. I mean we always seemed to end up at the Golden Corral. But, yet again, I was outnumbered. My suggestion was to possibly take it up a notch and maybe celebrate Dad's life together at some colorful Mexican restaurant. Nope. I was again shot down. And brimming with so many emotional feels and love after Dad's service, I realized I didn't have the fire to fight back. I took a "whatever" stance and let it go. They truly didn't want my opinion, and maybe for the first time ever, I didn't have the fumes to voice anything. So if "Silence is Golden," as the saying goes—the Golden Corral it was.

I was still reeling from the goodness I felt from so much of my extended family—my real friends, my adopted true family who accepted and loved me—who had shown up for me at the funeral. There were tons of them who hugged me and made me feel so cared for. Why was I doing headstands trying to win over those blood relatives when, in fact, I never really felt connected to them anyway? Nor they to me.

The truth is in my family, I have always felt like I was the outsider looking in. I simply didn't fit in, and somehow that was not a bad thing. These were not bad people—I just wasn't cut out of the same cloth as them. They were more of the conformist ilk, and as long as I could remember, all I wanted to do was live outside the lines. The rebel. I was and will forever be a freedom freak. I really was "born to be wild." Now, magically, I was discovering a clarity I'd never had before. A revelation: we are different from each other. Can we accept that? Wasn't it time to embrace those differences in a whole new way?

My incredible Life Coach, Connie Costa, is one of the great Healers in my world who has continued to balance me. She's helping me revisit that angry little girl tucked inside who was screaming to be recognized, validated, and understood. I loved my baby sister and brother back then; of course I did. I still love them to this day. But after a while, holding up the fort at home and caring for two overwhelmed, overworked parents——an emotionally broken mother and a furious father—and being a full-time babysitter and caregiver after eleven years of being The Only Child and loving all the time and attention I got, well, I had reason to be pissed off. I was too young to become a mother to all of them. My own childhood had been stomped on, suffocated, and tossed aside. I was a prisoner in more ways than one.

And now after my father's death, Connie was helping me discover all of that angst—and refocus it on LIFE. My life. Our lives. A fresh start. Leaving the past behind and forging a new and kinder reality I deserved. In fact we all did. Death to Life. It was time to be Reborn.

How to heal? I needed to document this journey, starting with my father's death into an entirely new existence of being. I decided to write this book to do what I have always loved doing—helping others. This book is our jumpstart place for the many retreats I hold—for the conversations, workshops, and podcasts I orchestrate to encourage others to explore their own Death-to-Life journeys.

Connie has acted as a Mediator between my sister, my mother, and me, encouraging us to face each other and our conflicts at last. You know this very well; the fact that if we don't resolve the battles within our own selves, they turn into an all-out war against our own bodies and each other. We fight dis-ease: all kinds of debilitating, diseased-filled health issues. And we ultimately die premature deaths fueled by festering fury. Remember that old adage, "Anger is like taking poison and hoping it kills the other person." Guess what, kiddos? We're the ones who are dropped by our poisonous perspectives.

So don't take the poison. Plant an inner garden instead. The one ready to be seeded with a wealth of health, beauty, and peace. It's okay to plant a real garden as well. Take in the wonder of life surrounding you. Trees. And flowers. And wildlife. Rivers and Oceans. The sky. The very air you're breathing right now. Bless it all. Open your own self-imposed prisons and throw away the key. It's time to be free! You are the one holding yourself hostage to hate, resentment, and the need to be right at all costs. Can you give that up now? As you see if I can, you can, too! Here's the thing. You really must if you want to live a joy-filled life.

Connie guided me to meditate, breathe, calm down, and truly understand the pain each of us in our family had experienced and how it all manifested to become such an incendiary timebomb. I recalled the fights between my parents, screaming out loud to my mother, "I don't want another child!" Mother had Fallopian tube issues after birthing me, and she was convinced she couldn't have any more children. And then boom! After an incredible vacation in Portugal (plus maybe the addition of a lot of wine-infused celebrating), Mother was miraculously pregnant. After eleven years! So the joy of welcoming one, then another baby was both a blessing and a curse for each of us.

Connie helped us listen to and love each other so much better through this renewed understanding. She gave us a homework assignment to acknowledge each other for thirty straight days. To love and forgive each other out loud no matter what. Seriously I've had easier assignments than this one.

During our individual and group healing work, I had this vision. I remembered this commercial I had loved so much as a kid. It was for the perfume Prince Matchabelli Aviance, and it featured a stunning woman who had this self-assurance I had never seen in a woman. I was around eleven when I saw her on TV—just perfectly timed around the blooming of Feminism, when women were being encouraged to burn their bras along with their subservient attitudes.

I loved everything about it—how that elegant, classy woman simply sauntered out of the kitchen where she was supposed to be a fixture and instead of cooking the bacon, she was possibly the one who was bringing it home by her own career and wealth, not dependent on anyone but herself.

Oh! How I wanted to be just like her. And now seeing myself from an entirely different POV, I saw that I have, indeed, become her. Even while raising four children and dealing with insane relationships and marriages, I became a Mayor, a business executive, a successful entrepreneur, and now a grandmother to six grandchildren and two great-grandchildren—a manifester of magic in all shapes and forms, including physical and spiritual wealth.

One of the many questions that have often bothered me is why women have been, and still are, thought to be so inferior to men. It's easy to say it's unfair, but that's not enough for me; I'd really like to know the reason for this

greatest injustice! Men presumably dominated women from the very beginning because of their greater physical strength; it's men who earn a living, beget children and do as they please...Until recently, women silently went along with this, which was stupid, since the longer it's kept up, the more deeply entrenched it becomes. Fortunately, education, work and progress have opened women's eyes. In many countries they've been granted equal rights; many people, mainly women, but also men, now realize how wrong it was to tolerate this state of affairs for so long. Modern women want the right to be completely independent!

—Anne Frank, thirteenth June 1944,
Diary of A Young Girl (the day after her
fifteenth birthday, approximately
two months before her capture)

And now my work is to help extricate each of you who are buried in the death process—figuratively and literally—and live on. Be LIFE. Truly our days are numbered. So why don't we count our blessings and beginnings—no matter how brief they may be—instead of fixating on the end game?

CHAPTER 7

NUMBERS RULE THE UNIVERSE

"Numbers rule the universe."

—Pythagoras

THE TRUTH IS human beings are many things associated with a whole bunch of abstract concepts poets, scientists, and spiritual masters have attempted for ages to try and define—such as an amalgamation of emotions, intelligence, creativity, and so much more. But beneath the surface of all that good stuff lies an undeniable truth. We humans—and the lives we live—are fundamentally composed of and hugely influenced by numbers.

Seriously we've allowed numbers to define us. Just think of it. Look at the medicines and vitamins, the liters of water (and other liquids!) we intake. They're based on numbers. From cholesterol levels and blood pressure to temperature and heart rate—everything reveals that intricate relationship between the mathematics of things to our very own human biology featuring our entire health and well-being.

We have all kinds of gadgets to regulate and monitor precisely the speed and length of our walks, runs, bike rides, swims, and mountain climbs—every and any sport we engage in. Documented by numbers. The winning and losing teams? Numbers. Ingredients for everything from cakes to casseroles? Numbers.

The produce we purchase at the market offers numbers to indicate freshness. Our scales show us the numbered truths of our weight (whether we like it or not!). The weather report gives us numbers of good and bad days—and the degrees of water, sun, snow, wind, etc., in terms of increments we can count on to be scary or sunny. We're lost without our calendars providing days, weeks, months, and years for us to track our place in time and space. And to that end, we're prisoners of the numbers of time allotted for doing what we want, need, or wish we didn't have time for at all. Consider all things financial that encompass the amount of money we have or don't have. Our mortgages. Our budgets. The cost of everything on the planet—from cars to housing to clothes, education—everything. How far or close are we to our goal? We tape measure, GPS, and time it all. All numbers.

Mainly there's the reality that we really can't avoid. Our days, weeks, months, and years we individually are allocated to live. Some infants live for bare moments, and there are those octogenarians who seem like God has forgotten them, and they live on into what looks like forever until they finally transition. Young age. Middle age. Old age. All numbers.

Or the countdown on the clock that tick-tocks away until everything simply stops. And you look at it the moment when your father takes his last breath and declare it to be 11:11. No matter that your other family members are screaming that it was, indeed, 10:49. My time. Their time. Lordy. Who CARES? What is time anyway? Try and define it. Can you see it? Hold it? Count on it to be dependable, illusive, or your reality or mine? I dare you to explain "time" to a child in a way that really makes sense. It doesn't. It's just a human attempt to measure our comings and goings—our height, weight, and seconds on this earthly plane—with some modicum of sanity in the face of what probably is all insanity anyway!

Being human may mean that our physical existence can be quantified by numbers, but we mustn't ever forget that we're each far more than the sum of measurements. We are each a lifetime of experiences, emotions, and intellectual capacities that are immeasurable, valuable, and precious. Sacred.

And no matter how much we wish to live forever, we can't. At least I believe not on Earth, but I am comforted to believe that we transition on to a Higher Place—a Heavenly Place—after we're unshackled from our bodies. You may believe something else, and that's cool. But this gives me great comfort in seeing the end as more of a beginning, rather than a permanent finale.

But no matter what our different beliefs are, there's one undying truth. Our time, in time, will run out. Our days and, indeed, our *lives* are numbered; everything has an expiration date. Our outer shells will break open, and our spiritual beings will be set free at last. The bodies we rattle around in for as long as we're here will ultimately wind down, break down, crash, crumble, or just screech to a grinding halt—peacefully or maybe not so much—and we simply stop and move on, returning back Home.

Because that's what being human is all about. Starting and stopping. Beginning and ending, accepting all the wonderful, horrible aspects of who we are in every way. Being human truly means facing the immeasurable truths that go way beyond the realm of numbers. Mathematics and measurements simply can't define us. No. Savoring every moment of life while we have it is what this earthly ride is all about. In the scheme of things, it's just a blink of a nanosecond when we're here and gone. Our possible mission, if we choose to accept it, is to love the brief, numbered moments we have while we have them.

Rabbi Shaul Marshall Praver encourages us to understand why we are far more than numbers. In his article entitled "The Photon and the Soul," he says,

Jewish practice prohibits counting people, lest it cause a plague. Accordingly, when Moses conducted a census, it was done by each person bringing a half shekel coin to the tabernacle and the Kohanim (Hebrew Priests) counted the coins. This is because counting quantifies and objectifies human beings. And since we believe the essence of a person is God's eternal spirit, a person is not the solitary image they appear to be and should not be counted in the manner in which objects are counted. There is so much about human beings that cannot be quantified.

This perspective is also necessary for world peace and planetary redemption. The greatest plague occurs when powerful people dehumanize less powerful people, because it lays the foundation for violence and unspeakable atrocities. Defamation always proceeds genocide. Whereas, when we see one another as non-quantifiable, non-objectifiable eternal souls holding God's transcendent presence, we will naturally safeguard human rights and the dignity due unto all creation. This perspective is needed for humanity to truly love and respect one another. The ramification of seeing every soul as a spark of God's eternal spirit, begets every admirable behavior needed for the flourishing of human civilizations. Just as the cosmos is interconnected and pulsating with energies undergoing various states of transformation, our degree of awareness ebbs and flows to the degree of our understanding and humble desire to learn more. Becoming sensitized to the spark of eternity encrypted in humanity and all of creation, prepares us to live transcendent lives. When this perspective is fully integrated into one's consciousness, the world and all that fills it will begin to reveal more of its secrets. This is the prophetic message of Habakkuk, "…

the earth will be filled with the knowledge of God as the waters fill the seas."

In conclusion, when this soul knowledge is fully integrated, and the hidden variables are revealed, transcendent consciousness will no longer seem the slightest bit mysterious. Soul consciousness will no longer be objectified as merely something good, but will henceforth be considered something that is simply true and essential for the survival of humanity.

—Rabbi Shaul Marshall Praver,
The Photon and the Soul

"Don't be afraid your life will end; be afraid that it will never begin."

—Grace Hansen

CHOICES

"Life is a sum of all our choices."

—Albert Camus

Just like the infinite outcomes in the Universe, we, too, hold a whole world of possibilities in our own hands. They're called "Choices." How are we going to deal with the burdens, challenges, roadblocks, seemingly dead ends, and mountainous climbs on our path? We choose. Positive over negative. Faith over fear. Love over hate. Peace over war. Hope over hopelessness. It's all up to us alone.

We take baby steps or huge strides on our paths and ultimately find the hidden gems along the way—if we're receptive to discovering them. The blessings. The "'Aha' moments" that lighten the load. We add positive results to those that have been subtracted and divided in our lives. We make the numbers total in our favor, and before we know it, we create ourselves to be "Numero Uno." And once we do that, I promise you, all the good that we seek and wish for in our own lives has this magical way of multiplying in exquisite ways to others.

The Universe may be packed full of numbers—but we don't have to be at their mercy. We need to remember our Humanity above all—our vision, heart, brains, and consciousness that make us more than unlimited mathematical options. And yes. You can count on it.

"A good decision is based on knowledge and not numbers."

—Plato

CHAPTER 8

WHAT'S NEXT AFTER ALL IS SAID AND DONE?

"Do not fall for categories. Everyone is everything. Every ingredient inside a star is inside you, and every personality that ever existed competes in the theatre of your mind for the main role."

—Matt Haig, *The Humans*

THE MORE I'VE journeyed into the chapters of my life, as well as those within this book, the more I look to the future with absolute hope and optimism. Even with all the time and energy I've had to go back there, into the conflicted, embattled recesses of my past, I've discovered that the journey from death to life is never truly over. Because, as I see it, we are all part of a greater Continuum. A journey that begins at the very end. Just like childbirth.

"Death is the start of a beginning, life is the start of the end, and the cycle continues forever."

—Tim Gurung, *Afterlife*

Birthing a baby is the oftentimes painful, messy labor that results in a beautiful child entering into the light after growing and evolving within a dark womb. The child often wails, gasping air into brand-new lungs. The mother is exhausted from the push-pull that brings her infant into the world—and so the adventure begins.

Many times the entire procedure isn't all that seamless. There's conflict, danger, excitement, fear, wonder, prayer—and so much more involved. Light after darkness. Bombarded with jarring noise after months of the soothing sounds of heartbeat and placental waters, being born can be shocking to a newborn. Can you imagine the questions we all have, suddenly awakening from that comforting place? Where am I? Why am I? What is this all about? Can I please go back? And really—if we're honest—we never stop wondering and trying to seek answers to those questions. I mean we're not born with a "How to Be A Human" manual. We must write it as we go. That's both a bummer and a blessing.

So that's how I see this Death to Life sojourn we're all traversing. It's far more than a passage of end to beginning. It's a reminder—if we allow ourselves to see it that way—for us all to live with intention, gratitude, and, yes, even a sense of urgency. This is our chance—before the endgame begins—to embrace our very existence and craft a life that reflects our deepest values and aspirations.

By truly acknowledging and very much embracing the profound duality of Death and Life—we're able to cultivate a keen understanding and appreciation of what it means to be human. Because death of a loved one forces us—even subconsciously—to face our own mortality, fostering a much greater appreciation for life and the recognition of its transient nature.

I have to admit that even though I pride myself in being a faith-filled individual who wholeheartedly believes in the meaning and magic behind all of life—I now have a much greater awareness of the fragility, the impermanence of everything. Going through all the highs and lows, that roller-coaster madness, as well as incredible sweetness of my father's dying process—all of it—has transformed me forever. I can even say that this whole experience—even with all the pain, fury, hilarity, and sorrow it's bubbled up in me—has been cathartic. Healing. It's been a kind of mirror holding up a recognition of who I really am and how can I be a better version of myself. I want to be better. I need to be better. I want to heal the wounds of my past relationships and rebirth more love than hate. To focus on what really matters, not what my ego tells me should matter.

"If light is in your heart, you will find your way home."
—Rumi

Death to Life is an extraordinary opportunity to travel way beyond the literal understanding of this entire process. Standing on the precipice of farewelling a loved one, we're actually able to delve much deeper into philosophical, psychological, and spiritual dimensions we never could have ever imagined before. Paradoxically this might have been my father's greatest gift to me; his last hurrah to help me grow up and learn the lessons of love and forgiveness on a greater, more astounding scale. His ending was and is my beginning. He turned the light on for me—as I believe we did for him, and he did for each of us in my family—and slowly we are learning to shine the light on each other. I haven't stopped saying, "Thank you, Daddy, for the infinite gifts you gave us all on this end/beginning sojourn."

CHAPTER 9

LESSONS LEARNED. LESSONS SHARED.

IT'S ALWAYS GOOD to stand back and be observers of our lives, as well as participants. No matter what you're going through now, or have slogged through in the past, it's a good practice to get into the habit of asking yourself these transformative questions, "What am I learning? What have I learned? What is my takeaway from this all?" And just like that, I promise you, the answers show up, loud and clear. Because when you stop to assess whatever is going on in your life, you instantly become a student, no longer a victim of circumstances. The added gift of stepping out of victimhood is that, almost immediately, you become a teacher of others. That's the magical journey of learning and sharing! So now let me share what I have learned and continually learn from my falling and getting up Death to Life passage:

1. **Gratitude.** Never stop saying and believing in the power of being grateful. If the only mantra you say over and over again—either inside your heart and mind or shouting it out

loud—is "Thank You," then you are celebrating the Gifts, not fixating and dumpster-diving into the Garbage.

2. **Heal.** Your inner child needs time, attention, and nurturing. You'll never be able to heal your grown-up wounds until you listen to and love the you who got lost by the roadside. Once you acknowledge your past pain, fear, and anger—validating those childhood feelings tucked inside—a brand-new adult you will emerge victorious on a path you could have never imagined waiting for you at last.

3. **Prepare.** Just like you're forced to get ready for an imminent birth (doctors and nurses, Midwife, baby shower, baby nursery, etc.), you need to go through all the steps necessary to get ready for your Death to Life experience—be it yours or someone else's. From finances to Hospice, to the who, what, and where of the burial process, to the Officiant, family, and friends invited, the order of the service—all of it taken care of with as many details as possible beforehand, making your life and that of your loved ones as seamless as possible when it's time.

4. **Anger.** Know that many of your tears of sorrow at this time will probably be mixed with a great deal of anger—for yourself and others, as well as the circumstance of shock, disbelief, helplessness, regret (and yes, relief as well,), etc., you might feel when not being able to stop or prevent the inevitable. Death is an integral part of Life. Once that fact is faced and dwelt with, we're far more able to harness, channel, express, and acknowledge anger—even expecting it to show up when it bubbles up. And it will.

5. **Sadness/Love-Hate.** Give yourself permission to ride the emotional roller-coaster that most of us face in the wake of the Death to Life experience. So cry, shout, and shake your fist to the heavens, do the "why me?" dance, and faceplant without knowing how or when you'll ever be able to get up

off the floor. My advice? Don't push it. You will be able to stand up and face the world but only in your time when you're ready. This is your very own Circadian Rhythm—not anyone else's. So give yourself a kind of deadline—be it daily, weekly, monthly, etc. "I need to feel sad for ___ amount of time. I need to cry or scream or be meditative or do everything I can to let myself be in this time and space." A good counselor, spiritual advisor, wise friend, life coach, etc., can really help shoulder your sorrow. I highly recommend reaching out to someone you trust with your heart. It's truly imperative now more than ever. In time Love will override everything, and if you let it—guided by compassion and renewed clarity—you'll be able to emerge stronger and wiser than ever before.

6. **Perspective.** Others in your life—siblings, children, extended family, friends, partners, etc., are experiencing their own shock, pain, anger, and memories that might not be in sync with yours. Guess what? It doesn't matter. Now is the time not to have to be RIGHT and make everybody else WRONG. You know that I am speaking from absolute experience on this one! Let them feel their own feels. Keep the door open to invite caring, sharing, hugging, and empathy, making this a time of healing, not added heartbreak. Just like my father kept saying our names over and over again so he wouldn't forget us, I am doing the same thing, saying my siblings' names over and over again so that I may be healed from and accept them as they are right now. It's amazing how positive the choice is to heal over hate when we're determined to create a far more meaningful and kinder life path.

7. **Release and Let Go.** There is tremendous truth in "Let Go, Let God." Even though we might think we have a handle on absolutely everything in our lives, the raw truth is that until we trust a Higher Power to help us, we're screwed. And you

can quote me. Only when I began asking—and TRUSTING—God and all my Angels to take some of my burden and give me the strength and vision to get through whatever I am facing was I able to see and feel the light of Hope embrace me. We simply cannot white-knuckle, tight-fist-clench our lives and expect anything positive to uplift us. Open-palm your life. Let go of those beliefs about yourself that might include being deserving of pain and abuse. They've only caused you more pain and setbacks that go nowhere but spiral into a hopeless abyss of self-deprivation, right? So let all that negativity and fear GO! Instead ask for help. We're not meant to tread this earth completely separate from each other. When we ask for—and provide—HELP, that's when the good stuff shows up. Release. Let Go. Rebirth. Rejoice. RETREATS!

HEALING RETREATS

Who could have imagined such a Death-to-Life rebirthing? Well, Jesus certainly did. And so this journey explores a similar path of personal redemption as I take you along with me. You each have your own stories dealing with death. Now is the time to discover them. I'm here to help you find your footing in a whole new reality after or amid whatever death experience you're going through at this very moment. As you can see, I've given myself permission to show up real, and I hope you do the same for yourself.

But you don't have to do this alone. I've designed some beautiful Angels Ranch Retreats for us to gather together and start fresh. My contact information as well as ways to learn about the retreats may be found below. In the past we've explored some astonishing life healings together at Angels Ranch Retreats—"Trust Love and Forgiveness," "Moving Magic Money," "Mystical Magical Arizona," and now our "11:11: A Journey from Death to Life."

Check my website for the details and do know that you can call me anytime for personal one-on-one coaching and LOVE!

I wish you blessings, love, and light, dear ones. The time is NOW. We've only just begun…

"WE'VE ONLY JUST BEGUN"
Song by Carpenters

We've only just begun to live
White lace and promises
A kiss for luck and we're on our way
(We've only begun)

Before the risin' sun, we fly
So many roads to choose
We'll start out walkin' and learn to run
(And yes, we've just begun)
Sharing horizons that are new to us
Watchin' the signs along the way
Talkin' it over, just the two of us
Workin' together day to day
Together
And when the evening comes, we smile
So much of life ahead
We'll find a place where there's room to grow
(And yes, we've just begun)
Sharing horizons that are new to us
Watchin' the signs along the way
Talkin' it over, just the two of us
Workin' together day to day
Together
Together
And when the evening comes, we smile
So much of life ahead
We'll find a place where there's room to grow
And yes, we've just begun

Songwriters: Paul Williams / Roger Nichols
We've Only Just Begun lyrics © Tratore, Universal Music
Publishing Group, Warner Chappell Music, Inc.

Kathleen Mello-Navejas
11:11: A Journey from Death to Life
P.O. Box 443
Huntington Beach, CA 92648
knavejas@verizon.net
1-928-233-2592

ABOUT THE AUTHOR

KATHLEEN MELLO-NAVEJAS

WHEN YOU STAND back, look at yourself, and ask who are you, it's amazing how the answers appear. Because we each are comprised of so many aspects—layers of categories, titles, and dimensions defining ourselves. The truth is we're not one thing. We're so many complex things—galaxies of things—into one-minute human forms. So as to the question who is Kathleen Mello-Navejas, I'm a French-Portuguese American—the first child of Carlos and Anna Mello, born in Fall River, Massachusetts, in 1954. I'm also a sister, wife, and mother. I've been a Mayor, presently a Healthcare Executive, and I have been blessed with four children, six grandchildren, and a great-grandchild. Five generations of powerful women who've created our astounding tribe! They are all very much a part of who I am. But I am also much more, including an author and—this is what I consider my greatest calling to be—a Healer!

I am so blessed to share this story, *11:11: A Journey from Death to Life*, with you. I fervently believe I'm meant to share this experience to help heal your pain, give you hope, laughter, and, most of all, *love*.

I constantly envision our time on this earth to be a powerful adventure of learning and growing from our challenges. That's my purpose—to help lift the curtain of fear, hopelessness, and despair you may be facing and do all I can to shift the vibration from negative to positive. There is indeed light at the end of the tunnel—and I am here to help you see and experience it.

It was a miracle that happened when losing my ninety-four-year-old father. I embraced a whole new life of unimaginable lessons from his death—rebirthing an entirely new perspective and reason for being on this earth. My father's end was truly my beginning and an epiphany to know what I need to enlighten you about your own Death-to-Life experience.

Even with his death, I was surprised by the amazing energy of peace and happiness I felt for that magical man, Carlos Mello Fagunda de Mello. After all that pain, sorrow, and vitriol I experienced, I have no regrets but rather sheer gratitude and laughter-filled joy, and the complete understanding that I was meant to share this experience with you. I want with all my heart to help you laugh through your tears and heal your soul and broken heart, as I was able to do, too. My dear father has helped me get to this place of peace and joy, and now it's my chance to give you these same gifts of healing and comfort.

I love you!
—Kathleen

ACKNOWLEDGMENTS

FIRST AND FOREMOST I acknowledge my father, Carlos Mello Fagunda de Mello, and the miracle numbers that he gave me: 3-23-2023 and 11:11, which have transformed me forever.

Dearest Dad, you made me who I am today—strong, powerful, fearless, and a true fighter for justice. I realize now that it was because of you that I have this fire in my belly and the courage to fight for empowerment and enlightenment.

It's your voice inside my voice that is guiding me to help not only myself but other women who need to believe in themselves, too. As I trust that I am enough, I am sharing this mantra and concept with others as well. No matter what we are more than enough.

The many challenges you gave me, Dad, gave me the strength to face them all and to do everything in my power to live a fearless, blessed life. God didn't make a mistake when he said, "This child is yours, Carlos." At times as a little girl, I saw the love you gave me, and it was magic. As I grew older, the tension and the rebellion showed up, and I fought you. I know now that you gave me the gloves to be the fighter I've become. I've needed to be strong, and you gave me that strength to get up off the floor after more faceplants than I could have ever imagined… I thank you with all my heart. I am who I am because of you. And for that I am grateful. You live on in me, Carlos Mello Fagunda de Mello—the Portuguese flag is flying high in my soul. You gave me the wings to know I really can fly. I. CAN. FLY!

Milton Keynes UK
Ingram Content Group UK Ltd.
UKHW020316211123
432926UK00001B/19